Loving Parents/
Happy Kids

Library of Congress Catalog Card No. 86-63128

ISBN 0-931722-53-5

Cover design by Patricia Broersma
Printed and bound in the United States of America

Loving Parents/ Happy Kids

A Team Approach to Child-Rearing

Ivan Fitzwater

A Publication of Management Development Institute

distributed by
Corona Publishing Co.
1037 South Alamo
San Antonio, Texas 78210

This book is dedicated to my teachers at the
Gaithersburg, Maryland, School from 1938-1950.
They taught love and discipline by example,
which is the very best way.

Contents

1. Stress Goals, Not Rules 1

2. Never Give a Kid a Second Chance 8

3. Prepare Children for the Real World 15

4. Avoid Rescuing, or, Who Owns This Problem? 21

5. Understanding the Causes of Behavior 27

6. Catch Them Doing Right 36

7. Prepare the Infant 43

8. Nurture the Rebelling Adolescent 51

9. Cooperate When Schools Discipline 57

10. Address Special Needs of the Gifted and Handicapped 66

11. Confront Drug Problems with Firmness 72

12. Use Physical Punishment Sparingly 80

13. Teach Personal Organization 86

14. Give Special Care in One-Parent Homes 93

15. Operate the Family as a Team 98

Addendum—Questions Parents Ask 106

Additional Readings 116

*Loving Parents/
Happy Kids*

Chapter 1
Stress Goals, Not Rules

If you had your choice, which would you prefer: a home where family members live happily, working together so that all achieve high goals, a home where children do chores and schoolwork without prodding—or a home where there is constant turmoil and conflict? Certainly the first home would be everybody's choice.

Why then do so few such homes exist? It is because the family has not consciously made a plan to cause these positive things to happen. Successful family relationships don't just happen—they result from commitment to fundamental principles which are embraced by the family members. This book describes a way of achieving a family environment where all are dedicated to control by self-discipline.

The problem with many approaches to establishing discipline in the home is that they start with rules instead of goals. Long lists of "don'ts" motivate creative children to devise ways to beat the system. Any child above the age of a few months can quickly become a legal scholar at finding loopholes and tying frustrated parents into technical knots.

Another problem with lists is that none is ever long enough to cover all possible circumstances. For example, a parent detects a strange odor coming from the child's room. Upon inspection, an aging cheese sandwich is found in a desk drawer. The parent's tirade ends with a question, "Why did

We have three simple goals
in our plan:

1.
All behavior must build the
individual.

2.
All behavior must build the
family.

3.
All behavior must be more than
fair to everyone.

you do a stupid thing like that?"

The reply is, "Nothing on your list says cheese sandwiches shouldn't be stored in desk drawers."

Let's stay out of two traps: 1) making decisions for children (where safety is not a concern), and 2) having parents and kids on opposite sides of the discipline issue. When parents make rules they actually take away from children the opportunity to learn self-management. They also put themselves in an adversarial stance in relation to their children. Neither of these gives the maximum chance for freedom, independence, and growth. We want a home where all family members have maximum freedom because all assume the level of responsibility which earns and warrants that freedom. The road to our dream is not paved with rules and parent/child conflict. What it does require is goals.

Goals will be stated in terms of the ideal. This can be a little scary to those who live in the real and imperfect world. Indeed, this could easily be the point at which some people put this little book down with disgust. Please don't! We have to have high goals to encourage maximum growth. Whether we actually achieve perfection (admittedly, no one will) is not the important thing. What is important is that we aim high, so our efforts aren't diminished by doing less than we can. Our efforts will assuredly make a bad situation better and an already good situation great by giving positive direction to our actions and relationships in the home and elsewhere.

At first the implementation of our plan will seem strange. We are so used to the typical power struggle between parent and child that departure from this atmosphere is uncomfortable. But our plan will be based on logical consequences rather than punishment of children by parents. In fact, our plan involves very little punishment at all! Parents will rarely have to punish. All family members will make choices and each choice will have a logical consequence which is assessed without exception. Consequences can be good or bad, pleasant or unpleasant.

The reason this approach will seem strange and unnatural at

first is because in most homes today things are done upon demand of the parents. The children's cooperation with these demands depends in large measure upon how well the demands match their desires. What we want to accomplish with our new plan is to cause children to make certain choices because these particular choices are best for all concerned and not simply the whim of parents. The parent will be relieved of responsibility for forcing, checking, and scolding.

Some adults may feel they are no longer being good parents when they adopt this procedure because their new role seems so much easier. This concern is understandable but without basis. Less control is better control when the result is responsible parents and kids.

We have three simple goals in our plan which provide guidelines for the behavior of all family members and constitute the framework of our program for establishing or restoring discipline in the home:

1. All behavior must build the individual.
2. All behavior must build the family.
3. All behavior must be more than fair to everyone.
   (Just fair is not enough; our plan encourages self-sacrifice as a fundamental and productive attitude.)

That's all there is to it; when everybody works toward these three simple goals our problems are over and harmony is achieved. We will have a home where there is happiness, little conflict, and maximum growth. Please note that *all* family members must work toward the goals, not just the children. The whole system breaks down when some family members opt not to participate. This will be obvious as specific instances are described in the chapters to follow.

This program is so simple that it is profound, but my experience tells me it is a long way from what is happening now in most homes. In some, conflict and self-destructive actions are constant. Even in successful homes family

It must be made clear

that the parents

will act as judges

but not as

police officers

on the beat.

members are not always acting in ways that allow maximum growth, and people who basically love each other occasionally act in unloving ways. These three goals can be the answer to restoring or improving the situation in either case.

To get started, it will take understanding and commitment on the part of all family members. I suggest a family meeting where the goals are openly discussed. I would hope this would be enough to get commitment, but if not, parents can institute the plan based on *understanding* by the children even if the goals are not agreeable to the children. If the parents do not embrace the plan, it is virtually doomed to failure. If they do, one step at a time, progress is made, and with each success future success is made easier.

The statement that all behavior must be more than fair to everyone will need special discussion. It is human nature to think of ourselves and our own needs first, and this causes conflict between people. The conscious effort of putting others first reduces conflict by setting a tone of conciliation. When this goal is embraced, family members are stretched in a positive, giving direction and any natural feelings of selfishness will be reduced.

Will there be setbacks and instances where the goals are violated? Certainly! Perseverance is essential to all real progress. But if the goals are constantly before us, we simply start again until failure is less and less frequent. When there is failure, the logical consequence pays the debt and the slate is wiped clean, thus making progress immediately possible with no lingering recriminations.

Now we are almost ready to begin, but before we do we must clarify the role of the parent or parents. Somebody has to have the final say in all matters and this must be a parent. In the family meeting it must be made clear that the parents will act as judges but not as police officers on the beat. Adults will listen, be fair in decisions, and as strict with themselves as with the children. Somebody must lead and decide fairly and with compassion—this is the parental role. It will be done without anger and with consistency which assures a minimum of stress on all concerned. All available evidence indicates that this is what children want anyway, at least in retrospect. It is like that teacher we remember with fondness. Chances are he or she was firm, fair, consistent, and compassionate. That teacher acted in such a way as to build us.

Now we have the simple goals in mind and we know the philosophy behind them. It is time now to discuss the specifics of putting our plan into action!

Chapter 2
Never Give a Kid
a Second Chance

My feelings, like yours, urge me to give children second, third, fourth chances and more, but this would be giving in to feelings that ultimately create an unfair, confusing world for them. It is these second chances, often given after great pleading on the part of children, that cause them to wonder whether or not consequences will really be assessed.

The gambling instinct is strong in all people. If there is a chance that the penalty or consequence won't be applied, the inclination is to take a chance. In our program, consequences are always assessed without exception.

I watched a mother and her four-year-old in a supermarket one day. The little boy would take items off the shelves, and the mother would rush to put them back. Each time she grabbed an item out of his hand she threatened a spanking. The boy knew she did not mean what she said so he continued to disobey at least seven or eight times. The mother then became quite angry and administered a rather severe spanking. I could see the wheels turning in that little boy's mind as he walked along sobbing. He had just learned that a few misbehaviors are all right but knowing how many times to misbehave would be his challenge.

The severity of the consequence has little to do with

The
severity of
a consequence
has little to do with
whether an act is repeated.
The thing that is crucial to
correcting behavior is the
inevitability of the
consequence.

whether an act is repeated. Severe punishment is often less effective than reasonable punishment because unfairness causes revolt where fairness won't. The only thing that is crucial to correcting behavior is the *inevitability* of the consequence. Every time a poor choice of behavior is made, there is a reasonable penalty which must be paid.

Penalties in life get harsher as we get older. How much better to learn while young, rather than later when penalties are very severe. Let me cite a few examples from everyday life to illustrate how inevitability of consequence is superior to severity of consequence.

Studies show that most motorists on the freeways today are driving above the legal speed limit. Why is this? The simple explanation is that very few speeders (as a percentage of all drivers) ever get caught. When drivers are apprehended, the penalties are severe, but since few get caught, most speed.

Let's suppose a system was devised which made punishment inevitable, even though the penalty was relatively mild. Suppose a device was placed on the dashboard of every car which recorded any speed over the limit. At inspection time, for example, the device would be read to see how many times the car went over the maximum speed allowed. I believe the problem of driving over the speed limit would be solved. The inevitability of a small fine every time a violation occurred would be more effective than the present situation where fines are severe but consequences are rarely assessed.

I grew up in a farming area in Maryland just as electricity was becoming generally available to the rural areas. This made possible electric fences to replace the tall wire and rail fences which were so hard to build and maintain. The electric fence was a single strand of wire at a height of about two and one-half feet off the ground, but it was far more effective than the old fences. This simplified fence gave a gentle shock every time an animal or person came in contact with the wire. The pain was enough to be unpleasant but not severe enough to do real harm.

The genius of the electric fence was that it gave a shock every time it was touched, with no exceptions. In spite of a simple sign which warned of the shock, I must admit I touched the fence because I was curious. It hurt and so it was a long time before I touched it again. Maybe it was my stubbornness, but a few months later I touched it again. It hurt me again. I don't recall ever touching it a third time.

It is normal to test our world to see what the consequences will be for certain behavior. It might even be considered normal to check a second time to see if the first consequence happened by chance. It is not likely that a behavior will continue to be repeated if the consequences are consistently painful. If that electric fence of my youth had only shocked periodically, I'd probably still be touching every fence that had a warning sign just because of normal curiosity and my gambling instinct. I would want to see if the sign really meant what it said.

In many respects, that electric fence was superior as a disciplinarian to many parents. The fence never threatened severe punishment. It did not become emotional but instead quietly applied inevitable consequences to all instances of undesirable behavior. The penalty was consistent and never unreasonable.

At this point someone may be thinking that I support physical punishment as a consequence. This is an incorrect interpretation because, as I will explain later, I rarely recommend physical punishment and only under very strict and limited circumstances. The point of the electric fence analogy is the concept of limited consequences on a completely dependable basis. This concept is what I hope the reader will grasp. Let me demonstrate the concept in a situation where physical punishment is not used.

A young boy or girl of fourteen is fully aware that the family has adopted a curfew for children of that age. A family discussion had been held and agreement reached after all family members had their say. The fourteen-year-old comes in

Reasonable consequences
assessed in an
atmosphere of love
and applied without exception
will correct behavior
while leaving the dignity of
the child
undamaged.

an hour after deadline. The parents take note of the violation and decide that next week the child must be in an hour before curfew as a consequence. Not a severe punishment, but one that not only fits the violation but has been assessed in an atmosphere of respect and love.

If children are to act in a way that builds themselves (the first of our three goals), they must get their proper rest and not be out at an hour that brings them into contact with temptations and dangerous situations beyond their maturity. Most parents recognize this but in trying to improve and correct the behavior, they act too severely or inconsistently, leading the child to gamble against the system or fight back against unreasonable punishment.

"You were an hour late," yells the parent. "Just for that, you are grounded for two months."

The penalty given in anger is too harsh and the child knows it. The reaction will be anger and a determination to fight back against the loss of dignity. The likelihood is that the child will challenge the unfair penalty by going out without permission or by manipulating the parents into a second chance—in other words, no penalty. The future becomes clouded because neither parent nor child knows what to expect. Reasonable consequences assessed in an atmosphere of love and applied without exception correct behavior while leaving the dignity of the child undamaged. This also minimizes the defiance of parental authority and the manipulation of adults by their offspring. These lofty ideals are quickly undone by harshness and unpredictability.

This is why I say a reasonable consequence must be applied every time. We undo ourselves the very first time we give our kids a second chance.

At the risk of being redundant, let me add one additional thought. Parents must stay out of the business of punishing as much as possible because this puts parents and kids in adversarial positions. Everything that happens to a child—good or bad—is his or her choice.

"You chose not to weed the garden, so you have chosen not to go to the movies." This keeps the emphasis where it belongs and prevents the parents from being bad guys. Parents simply judge the choices made by children and administer the consequences which were decided upon in advance by a loving family team.

Chapter 3
Prepare Children for the Real World

The greatest act of love is to never do anything for children which they can do themselves. Think of it this way: When parents do for them what they are capable of doing, children become dependent. I call it the welfare system. Able people who are made dependent generally resent the one who provides for them, no matter how noble the intent.

When parents do too much for their children it is usually because of their ignorance of what helps children grow best. In some cases it is because of a parent's guilt feelings in some other area of the relationship or it may be because parents get enjoyment from giving without realizing their joy is at the expense of the children.

"We gave them everything so they wouldn't have to work as hard as we did and they don't seem to appreciate it at all." This is a statement commonly heard from disappointed parents. They don't realize that when they were working hard as they grew up, they were getting from it a feeling of self-worth because of their contributions to the family and their own independence. Many children today are virtually on welfare when it comes to their own needs and they don't feel essential to the success of the family as a whole. Additionally, since this is the only system they have known, they grow to

The greatest act of love is to never do anything for children which they can do for themselves.

expect a world which caters to their needs.

To prevent these problems, we must prepare children for the real world. They will in no way be exploited in what they are required to do, but neither will they be crippled by having too much done for them. In the real world you are expected to do for yourself everything which is possible. You are expected to contribute for what you receive. Adults who go to work get wages; those who choose not to, don't get paid. Nobody shouts, screams, or chides either way. In fact, the world doesn't seem to care. This system of logical consequences out in the world forms the basis for the preparation of children for that world. Some illustrations of this may clarify what I am proposing.

Each family member has certain chores assigned based on his or her maturity and obligations outside the home. Bed making, lawn care, dishes, pet feeding, laundry, etc., would be typical of these assignments. The assignments are made after family discussions to assure fairness and understanding; some may be on a rotating basis. When the obligations are met, privileges are given: television watching, talking on the phone with friends, weekly allowance, etc. When obligations are not met, privileges are not available. The parents act as final judge (including holding themselves to high standards), deciding to what degree work has been accomplished.

There is no pleading or reminding done by parents and there is no emotion when judgements are made except possibly some praise for work done exceptionally well. Privileges are only withheld until the work is done and there are no extra penalties or punishment as reprisal. Trading of assignments is permitted (as approved by parents) because this is the way the real world works. If a family member is temporarily incapacitated or experiencing extra obligations outside the home, other family members are encouraged to go the extra mile to help out. This is done on a reciprocal basis with no one taking advantage of the situation. Every family member gets a feeling of earning his or her way. No one is on welfare. Being part of the team reminds the children of their importance and they grow and learn skills necessary for their own independence.

Family members are expected to meet their obligations without monitoring or reminders by others in the family. Getting up on time, leaving for work or school with the proper materials necessary for work is the responsibility of each individual. In the case of kindergarten and first-grade children an older family member will make sure the child is thoroughly awakened. Mastering the important life skill of meeting personal obligations is important for individual success and family harmony. To deny a capable person the opportunity to assume such responsibility would be an insult.

In the family meeting it is agreed that each family member will be responsible for meeting his or her own obligations. If the school bus is missed there will be no rides to school in the family car. Forgotten lunches or gym suits are not taken to school by parents. The child who misses the bus may ask for an exception to be made (especially if parents had bailed them out in the past) but the reply is, "I love you too much to insult you by doing for you what you can do for yourself."

Does this sound harsh? Think about it. In the real world, if you miss an airplane, do the airlines call up a smaller plane to carry the late passenger? Certainly not, and no one expects them to. Many children miss buses today because they know there is a backup system to make up for their tardiness.

The child who misses a bus might walk to school if it is safe or miss a day and have to call a friend to catch up on assignments. It is not likely this child will continue to miss the bus if he or she is sure there will be no special rides in the family car. This important lesson is best learned at a young age when the penalty is only a missed day of school or a long walk, rather than the loss of a job.

Learning to work as part of a team and meeting one's own obligations are two extremely important concepts essential for success and happiness. Recently, I read in the newspaper that people who held jobs as youngsters were consistently more successful than those who did not. I sincerely believe this is

Family members are expected to meet their own obligations without monitoring or reminders by other family members. Getting up on time, leaving for work or school is the responsibility of each individual.

true. Adults, in addition to setting a good example in their own lives, must provide opportunities for children to learn responsibility. It is sad but true that many young adults in high school and college cannot operate a washing machine or prepare their own food or get themselves to class on time. Their lives are miserable because the parents aren't there to prevent or assume the consequences. The adult world can be harsh to those who haven't been educated to its realities.

Chapter 4
Avoid Rescuing, or,
Who Owns This Problem?

The one who supervises least, supervises best. The ultimate goal of our program to achieve loving parents/happy kids is self-discipline where no monitoring is necessary. If control has to be external, it will break down. No system of monitoring can be constant. Punishment enters the system only as a logical consequence of a particular behavior.

The path to achieving this state of self-discipline has been described in the previous chapter, but now we must give particular attention to the most serious threat to our success with the program—the urge to rescue.

The urge to solve someone else's problem is a normal one. Most people are magnanimous and kindhearted by their very nature but this urge is even more acute when one feels he or she has superior knowledge compared to another. Business managers solve problems for their employees and then wonder why the same employees can't take charge of their jobs and become decision makers. School principals handle the misbehavior in a teacher's classroom rather than educating the teacher to be a disciplinarian, and the stream of referrals to the office grows rather than diminishes. Parents step in where children could solve their own problems rather than helping the children become problem solvers.

When someone close to us
has a problem,
we can avoid
harmful rescuing by asking
ourselves these questions:

1.

Who owns this problem?

2.

What can I do that will be
most helpful in the long run?

The solution must be to consciously avoid unnecessary injury or irreparable damage but we must support, not rescue. The people we love are going to suffer pain which we could prevent, but this is done to avoid a greater pain in the future. We have to make a special effort, show special courage to avoid rescuing, and thus hurting, in the long run, those we love.

When someone close to us has a problem, we can avoid harmful rescuing by asking ourselves these two questions: 1) Who owns this problem? and 2) What can I do that will be most helpful in the long run? Quick fixes often do more long-term harm than good. For example, a child gets into trouble in school. The parents know that they have political influence with important school officials and could prevent any punishment of the child. If they exercise the influence and prevent the fair punishment, the child may get the notion that he or she is above the law. The parents wisely decide not to interfere so the child learns a lesson. This is a tough stand for the parents to take, but they are considering in the long term what will be best for their child. This leaves them in a much better position to intervene in a situation where the punishment might be unfair.

Who owns the problem? If it is ours, then we go about solving it in the most productive way. If we determine that the problem is owned by someone else, then we try to play a productive role in helping the rightful owner solve the problem. This puts us in a counseling role which involves listening—lots of listening, not preaching or providing our solution to the problem. Only the owner of the problem can provide the solution. We listen but do not give answers. Our listening and questioning help the other person find the best answer.

Our listening and questioning will likely be most productive if it is structured rather than random. The basic model of the structure involves three questions. If we can get the other person to consider these three questions, he or she will know what must be done to solve the problem.

1) What is the problem?
2) What are my alternatives?
3) What will be the consequences of each choice?

Once an individual has thoughtfully answered these questions, the best answer should evolve. A counselor (often a parent) can provide the structure and compassionate listening which insure a conducive atmosphere for this scientific approach.

When we successfully lead someone to a solution to his or her problem by using the three questions or steps, there will normally be a high commitment to the plan. If we *give* someone our solution, unconsciously that person will be less committed and will likely give less effort to carrying the plan to fruition. There may even be resentment of the solution if it comes from outside.

As you are counseling a young person or anyone who has never been systematic in problem solving, be patient. When you ask, "What is the problem?" there may be great thrashing around. It may be that the thing which was thought to be the problem is not the problem at all.

"My teacher doesn't like me," is the first interpretation. But after consideration brought on by probing, sympathetic questions, it turns out that the problem is that the student talks too much in class. Obviously a solution based on the first asumption would have been wrong.

The same is true with solutions. At first there may be many, but after you listen the person says, "I can see that this is the thing I should do." The power of compassionate listening has caused the best answer to surface.

Thus far I have been discussing how to avoid rescuing after a problem has developed. There is another dimension worthy of our consideration and that is how to prevent the need for rescuing by the way young people are reared. As infants and children, their experiences can contribute to an attitude of self-sufficiency which creates a larger than normal feeling of self-confidence.

*If we can get the other
person to consider
these three questions,
he or she will know
what must be done
to solve the problem:*

*1.
What is the problem?*

*2.
What are my alternatives?*

*3.
What will be the
consequences of each
choice?*

I recommend that parents consciously provide experiences designed to develop in the child high self-confidence and independence. This must start at a very young age—far younger than many would imagine. We must fight the notion that any child is too young to take charge of responsibilities. We must let them do things without criticizing the way they do them and we must fight the urge to do things over just because we can do them better.

Even one- or two-year-olds have a natural urge to help. Let's respond to this urge. If they put away their toys, we compliment them, even though the job isn't perfect or done the way we would do it. We must keep in mind that our goal is to develop children who are self-sufficient, not to have perfect toy storage. They will become more competent if we give them time and encouragement rather than criticism. The work is not the important thing. It is the child's image of self.

Children must be allowed to do exciting jobs which they see adults doing, not just garbage details and drudgery. If they want to help cook, let them. You may get some strange meals for a time, but they will be developing a can-do attitude. When you paint the house, let each one do his or her own room with the least amount of help possible. You will be painting it again in some years anyway. Here is a chance for a child to develop high self-esteem. I suspect the child will take better care of the paint in that room if he or she did the work.

Preventing the need for rescuing and then handling situations constructively without rescuing when problems do occur will build good human relationships. It takes conscious effort and an overcoming of our natural tendency to rush in with short-term cures, but it is essential to real growth and happiness. It is also the best way to show true love for another person.

Chapter 5
Understanding the Causes
of Behavior

Teachers and other professionals who work with young people over a period of time get to the point where they can pretty much predict what the parents are like by observing the behavior of children. The reverse of this is also true. When the behavior of parents is known, it is possible to predict what the child will be like. Let me cite a few fictitious examples.

Low Freedom + High Love = Rebellious Child

John and Mary expressed their love for their children by being very strict parents. They made all of the decisions for their children, chose their playmates, picked out their clothes, and provided for their every need. There was no question that they loved their kids and, in fact, that the kids seemed to mean everything to them; everyone referred to them as devoted parents. The combination of a tight rein and obvious love worked pretty well when the kids were small, but as they grew older there started to be conflicts. When the children became teenagers, they rebelled completely and finally the parents lost control.

Low Freedom + Low Love = Deceitful, Sneaky Child

Sam was a single parent so he tried to make up for what he considered was a loss for his children by being a strict parent. He tried never to let the kids out of his sight, but when he was with them, he never really got close to them. It seemed as though the children were a burden to him and he didn't communicate feelings of love. The children reacted by becoming deceptive and sneaky because this was the only way they could figure to get their unloving parent to give them some of the freedom they desired.

High Freedom + Low Love = Runaway Child

Eleanor and Pete were so wrapped up in themselves and what they were doing that they really didn't have time for their kids. It was pretty obvious the children were a bother. There was no affection shown in the family, and little time spent with the children. The kids could come and go as they liked. But since the home was a very unpleasant place, they did not feel attracted to it. At a very early age they ran away from home in search of love and a more stable environment.

High Freedom + High Love = Secure, Independent Thinker

Harriet was a widow who recognized that children thrive on obvious love. She told her son and daughter that she loved them, quite frequently, and she backed up her words with her commitment to their well-being. Her philosophy was that children should be given every bit of freedom that they can handle and that they earn. She discussed with her children the options that are available in life and the consequences which go along with the choices. She didn't try to live her children's lives for them. Instead, she counseled with them and, whenever possible, supported

High
Freedom

+

High
Love

=

Secure,
Independent
Thinker

their choices. In this environment of high love and maximum freedom, the children flourished and became leaders in their own right.

These examples are not intended to be definitive or absolute on the topic of childrearing. Instead, they are illustrations of how behavior of adults impacts on the behavior of children. The examples are sharply delineated with the understanding that in reality there are shades of gray. The behavior of most parents would fall somewhere in between the categories. Still, these examples can speak to us in terms of helping us understand why children do the things they do.

As loving parents who are trying to rear happy kids, we must find ways to give them maximum freedom to make choices in an atmosphere which assures them that they are loved. This is our best chance of getting them ready for life so they will be highly motivated to do the things which are best for them. Unfortunately, the things we need to communicate cannot be taught in a traditional way. Some of what we want to communicate can be done by talking and explaining, but there are other techniques which will be far more effective. Most of what children internalize and thus what ultimately affects their behavior comes from the covert messages from adults and from imitation.

Covert Messages

To a great degree, children become what we think they are. This is because our judgements of them become their self-fulfilling prophecies. Over-protective parents generally have children who have a lot of accidents. The reason for this is very obvious. The message that the child hears constantly is, "You're going to have an accident." This makes the children more tense, and when they get more tense, they have more accidents. The parents then respond by saying, "See, what did I tell you?"

If we want children to have confidence in themselves, we must show we have confidence in them. If we want them to be

To a great degree,
children become
what we think they are.
The reason for this
is that
our judgements of them
become their self-fulfilling
prophecies.

able to handle freedom, we have to show them that we think they can handle freedom by giving them more freedom. The labels that we place on children can become their goals. "Oh, you are so clumsy. You are always knocking things over," says the parent in disgust. The child absorbs the message and carries out the prophecy by being very clumsy. All through his or her life, the child has an expectation of clumsiness.

The covert message becomes a reciprocal thing because it sets up an expectation which is then fulfilled and leads to another expectation in the same direction. Some years ago, a teacher in junior high school was given the locker numbers of children instead of their IQs. It happened that these lockers were all in the 120 wing of the school, so the teacher thought she had very talented learners, even though they were all average or below on their real IQ scores. The teacher expected the children to do well and they did, and by the end of the semester the grades were very high. The teacher couldn't believe it when she found out that the IQ scores were really below average. She had set up an expectation and the children responded to it and became much more productive than they were under the previous labels.

Imitation

Children are natural imitators so the impact of modeling by adults is profound. When children are very young, parents are heroes who the children assume are superior to all human beings. Little kids think their dad can beat up any other dad on the street and that their mother is prettier than any other woman. In adolescence, young people start imitating each other and this gives rise to what is known as peer pressure. But it is still the urge to imitate.

To adults who are trying to make a positive effect on young people's behavior, this means that we will see ourselves reflected in our children. If I exercise and otherwise take good care of my health, the children will imitate it. If I go to church, rather than just sending my children, the likelihood is they'll take church more seriously. If I take pride in obeying the law, so will they. If I am optimistic and positive, then they will be too. Unfortunately, the reverse of all these positive examples is true also. If I treat myself poorly, or if I am negative toward the world, this will also be imitated.

At this point I would like to call particular attention to a certain trend in parenting. Many parents put themselves last and do everything for their children. While the motivation behind this idea is very noble, it is not a good example for young people. In the last analysis, the children are probably going to treat themselves the way we treat ourselves as adults because of the imitation. We must make sure that we keep balance in the family and have an equal sharing of benefits and hardships.

Having made the strong point about covert messages and imitation and the effect of these on children's behavior, now it is time to note the exception to the rule. We have been talking in general terms about the two major concepts which really mold the behavior of young people: covert messages and modeling. Occasionally, however, we will run into the phenomenon of overreaction. It works this way.

Let's suppose that both parents are heavy cigarette smokers and as the children grow up they are used to riding in an automobile filled with this smoke. The response to this is so negative that it actually results in an overreaction in later life, and the child of two parents who are heavy smokers may become a dedicated nonsmoker. The same might be true with the drinking of alcohol. The child of alcoholic parents will, on occasion, overreact and become a teetotaler. The child who grows up under parents who use severe corporal punishment might overreact and never use physical punishment on his or her children.

Such examples of overreaction are rare, but on occasion they do occur. As parents, though, we cannot count on overreaction. For the most part, we have to depend on sending positive, covert messages and providing good models rather than telling them, "Do as I say, but not as I do."

Now that we have reviewed the major causes of behavior in children, it might be well to conclude this discussion by defining in more detail what we are looking for as an outcome. I've already stated that we want a child who can exercise self-discipline and thus deal with the independence that adulthood brings. As we watch the child developing, it would be well to keep in mind that the goals we are seeking will be accomplished in the greatest degree if the young person is assertive rather than passive or aggressive. Unfortunately, the behavior of most young people will fall predominately into the passive or aggressive categories. Let's take a closer look at these three categories of behavior.

Passive Personality

Children come into the world with an instinct for aggression. The young child will reach out and take away another's toy. When they learn to talk they say what is on their mind, no matter who is listening. Parents naturally have to control these behaviors if the child is to get along in a social environment, but some parents go too far, and they educate the child into passiveness.

The same is true of schools. The children have to stand in line and hold up their hands before they speak, and there are admonishments when these rules are violated. As parents, we have to be very careful that we don't go too far in talking about politeness and letting others have their way. There is a delicate balance between politeness and fairness on the one hand and becoming so passive that others can take an unfair advantage.

Aggressive Personality

When the child has not received enough experiences in the socialization process to become a team player, he or she may develop a "bully" personality. The aggressiveness is often exacerbated by low self-image brought on by lack of love from others in the environment. If properly channeled, this type of personality can sometimes become a leader. More often it can lead to hostilities with authority figures and with the rules that are often necessary in a cooperative living relationship such as a school.

Assertive Personality

The constellation of behaviors that we are seeking fall neither in the passive nor in the aggressive categories. What we want is a blend of the two, where the individual has enough aggression to stand up for what is rightfully his or hers, but never goes beyond that point to take advantage of other people's rights. This personality puts the individual forward in a wholesome way but not in a way that is repugnant to other people.

It is obvious as we look at the broad categories above that we want to rear children who have assertive personalities. Bearing in mind that children learn most through covert messages and imitation, this means that we, as adults, must live assertive lives. We stand up for what is rightfully ours and we defend the rights of other individuals. We must demonstrate fair play and the golden rule in everything that we do.

It's a big challenge, but then nobody ever said that parenting was going to be easy.

Chapter 6
Catch Them Doing Right

In most homes a child can do 99 things right, and never hear anything about it, but let him or her do something wrong just one time out of 100 and they never hear the end of it. This same phenomenon has been observed in the world of business, in our schools, and indeed in society in general. The natural tendency is to call attention to the things which are wrong, rather than noticing the things which are right. This is the way the world works. If the psychologists are right that people grow when their strengths are identified, then this negative approach is not the best way to improve behavior.

One of our three goals in the development of loving parents and happy kids states that everything we do must build other people in the family. To fulfill this goal and in light of what we know about building on strengths, we must make a conscious effort to call attention to the things which are done right and at the same time we must curtail our tendencies to be critical of the things done wrong. Once again, this is going to seem strange and unnatural because our environment will not be working that way.

Children tend to repeat the behaviors that adults call attention to, whether these behaviors are good or bad. When we notice the things that children do wrong, we actually encourage the repeating of the act. Children quickly learn this and actually use it as a manipulative technique. They realize that when they act in a certain way, their parents are going to react in a certain way, so they punch the button to get the attention which they desire.

For example, two small children are playing together and one of them feels that things are not going just the way he or she would like. So the child throws a tantrum which immediately brings all of the adults into the situation as they rush to intervene on behalf of the crying child. Rest assured this behavior will be repeated any time the child wants the assistance of the adults.

There are three guidelines that I would suggest we follow as we attempt to catch our children doing right:

1. Treat Children As You Would
A Good Neighbor

When the good neighbor next door lets the lawn go uncut for a couple of weeks and we begin to wish that they would spruce things up, we don't say anything about it. When they do finally get around to making things tidy, we compliment them on how good it looks. If our neighbor falls down while skiing and breaks a leg, we don't go over to his house and punish him for not being careful. We would never say, "If you had been home here doing what you should, this wouldn't have happened. You obviously were not being careful enough. Now I'm not mentioning this for *my* own good, you see. I knew better than to break my own leg. Maybe this will teach you to be more careful next time." These kinds of statements sound ridiculous when we are talking about a loving neighbor, but they are the very things that we say to our children.

We can continue this analogy of our relationship with our neighbor to help us understand what we should do when a child's room is messy. In the case of the neighbor, things would have to look pretty bad outside before we would say

Children tend to
repeat the behaviors
that adults call
attention to,
whether
these behaviors are
good or bad.

anything, and we would never make reference to untidiness inside their home.

Let's do the same thing with the child who has a messy room. If the untidiness spills over into the den or the living room of our home, then we have a right to say something if this becomes a pattern or is severe. But as long as the rest of the house is tidy, children can leave their own room any way they want. When they do anything to improve the condition of their room, we praise them for it. Other than that, we set a good example in our own rooms, and eventually they will follow the example. This approach will prevent much of the conflict that occurs between parents and children.

2. Be Positive Even When They Fail

Children grow and improve when they keep trying, so the real challenge for parents is to keep them trying. When they fail and we criticize them for it, or we immediately step in and do something for them, their bent toward trying is diminished.

All people grow best in an atmosphere where failure is permitted and willingness to try is praised. The small child tries to tie his or her shoe, but just can't seem to get it right. The wise parent says, "You put your shoes on all by yourself and you are learning to tie your shoes. I'm proud of you." The emphasis is upon what the child has done well, the putting on of shoes, and attention is given to the child's trying to learn to tie the shoes. The likelihood is that this child will try again. But if we had said something like, "Oh, you are doing it all wrong," the willingness to risk would have been damaged.

An older boy or girl goes out for a place on the team or a part in the school play but is not successful. The wise parent says, "I'm pleased that you tried and gave it your best effort. That kind of attitude is going to lead you to many successes in life." And what could have been seen as failure suddenly is looked upon as success.

One of the most difficult places for parents to remain positive when children fail is when the report card is brought home from school. If there is any low or failing grade, the

There are three guidelines to follow as we attempt to catch our children doing right:

1.

Treat children as you would a good neighbor.

2.

Be positive even when they fail.

3.

Avoid effusive praise.

tendency is to call attention to it first and demand an explanation. A better way would be to look at the report card and first notice anything that is positive. It might even be wise to let the child explain how the success was achieved in these areas. When it comes time to discuss the failing grade, there is a positive foundation from which we can start. "You did very well in social studies and you told me how you did it. What are you planning to do in algebra that will make your efforts more successful there?" This approach will be much more productive in improving the algebra situation than would a discussion of what caused the failure.

3. Avoid Effusive Praise

In giving praise, it is important to keep from going overboard so that the praise becomes an end in itself. It is best to simply make a positive statement about what is good, rather than inducing excess emotion which can become hypnotic. When the grade on the report card is improved over the previous marking period, we can become so excited in our praise that the student gets the idea that this is good enough. It will produce much more growth if we simply make a comment about the positive progress, such as, "You are making improvement, and I'm pleased. And I bet you will continue to improve." This catches the child doing right, but at the same time, keeps him or her growing.

It is amazing to observe the growth that is possible when the child experiences an environment that is totally positive. In my lectures to teachers, I ask them to try what I call the "positive list" experiment. Each teacher has the students write down everything that they are capable of doing. Then the lists are turned in to the teacher, and of course there are not many items listed. The teacher then reminds them of all the additional things that they are good at, such as telling stories or singing or doing errands. The lists are given back and the students add all the additional items they can think of. The teacher encourages the students to help each other by pointing out to their classmates the things that they know that others do well so that they can build their lists too. Students also are asked to have their parents and brothers and sisters help them list things they can do. Never is anyone permitted to mention something that another person cannot do.

As the days pass, the lists keep growing, and the enthusiasm builds. Teachers have told me that parents on the way to work would suddenly think of something that the son or daughter could do and they'd stop the car and call the school from a phone booth so the item could be recorded. The conversations around the dinner table at home were directed toward discovering other things that should be added to the list.

Not only does this put the emphasis on the positive in life, but teachers tell me that during the positive list experiment, behavior in the classroom improves, school achievement increases, and interpersonal conflicts are just about nil. What is happening is that all of the other human beings around any given child are trying to catch the youngster doing right.

In summary, people work best and grow more when recognition is given to their achievements. I think many of us can remember how hard we tried never to miss a day at Sunday School so we could get the gold star at the end of the year. As adults, we are still giving extra effort so that our ego needs will be met as others in the world recognize our achievements.

It is true at any age of development, but particularly true for children: We repeat those things that cause our emotional needs to be met. As parents and teachers, we can cause wholesome behaviors to be repeated by taking extra care to notice every time a child does something right.

Chapter 7
Prepare the Infant

Infancy (roughly the first three years) is a crucial time for doing the things necessary for the development of a secure individual who has a wholesome image of self and of the world in general. It is also a time to protect the child from trauma and other forces which sow the seeds of maladustment later in life.

Parents who want their children to embrace strong religious convictions must instill those convictions during these early years or it is unlikely that parental influence will determine these convictions. The saying "Give me the child and I'll give you the man (woman)" has scientific basis.

Preparation for a secure infancy begins even before birth. Good nutrition on the part of the mother and abstinence from addictive substances are imperatives because these affect the baby's ability to adjust to the shock of leaving the womb. The smoother the transition, the easier it is for the infant to adjust to the changing rhythm of life and the new stimuli which occur at birth.

For the quickest and least traumatic transition, the new environment should emulate the womb as much as possible, especially just after birth. The child should be held a great deal so that the warmth and the heartbeat of the parent's body can be sensed directly. The act of nursing, with the intense physical contact, is also quite beneficial. The only way the infant has to signal discomfort is by crying. Attention must be given to the cause of the crying until the child is calmed. Hunger, wetness, pain—whatever the cause, it must be addressed and solved. "Letting the infant cry" was a theory of childrearing which was very popular at one time. There is nothing in current research to support such a technique. The infant needs love expressed in any and every possible way.

Many books have been written about the child in infancy. Our concern here is not to offer instruction for parents in all of the important areas of childrearing, but rather to address several areas which seem to have special impact on the way the child responds in later years.

Bedtime

Infants respond well to a routine so it is important that a bedtime routine be established. This should not be an absolute schedule with no variations, but it is helpful to have a regular bedtime with a happy sequence of events— something that is anticipated with pleasure rather than dread. It should not be a hurried time.

A relaxing bath where parents play with the baby is a good idea. A bedtime story with laughter and singing makes it a happy time. Too much excitement should be avoided, however. An emphasis on quiet activities as sleep approaches is recommended. If the child is extra tired, more rocking and holding may be necessary. If sleep does not come after normal routines, extra time may be necessary with the infant. Should the child ever use this as a manipulative device, this can be overcome by staying with the child but discontinuing bedtime activities. This shows love but maintains control at the same time.

Mealtime

We have all known children who have somehow been able to manage their parents at mealtime. Stubborn refusal to eat results in increased parental stress, as the little one just sits until the parents give in. "Eat just one more bite," is often the last effort to maintain a semblance of control which both parent and child know is really acquiesence.

There is a better way, one which results in no anger or show of strength on the part of the parents, but still raises a healthy, responsible child. As is so often true in childrearing, the best way is also the easiest way, but it doesn't seem natural and it takes perseverance.

The family team prepares the food and sets the table, with even infants participating as appropriate to their capability. Meals are served at about the same time each day so they become a comfortably scheduled event. Great variation in meal times is sure to interfere with someone's plans and this means potential conflict.

A wholesome diet is provided for everyone. Requests for certain foods are considered by the parents and these requests are accommodated where possible, but the loving parents make the final decision. Food is served and all are given sufficient time to eat. Mealtime should be a happy time of family togetherness and not a time for Mom and Dad to resolve differences or to discuss weighty family matters. Dessert is a bonus for those who eat in a reasonable time. Any who don't eat the basic food thus choose to forego dessert or any other food until the next mealtime. There is no shouting, no begging, no show of anger.

In this environment, children soon learn to choose to eat what is provided because of the rewards which accompany such a choice. The first time a parent gives in and allows dessert or a snack "just this one time" the battle is lost because infants learn they can manipulate adults and get their own way.

Tantrums

Very young children can be quite creative in the ways they attempt to control adults. Holding their breath, screaming (especially in supermarkets where parents are embarrassed), and stubborn stoicism are typical tantrums, particularly of the terrible two-year-olds. This is a critical time in parenting

A*ny who don't eat*
the basic food
thus choose to forego
dessert or any other food
until the next mealtime.
There is no shouting,
no begging,
no show of anger.

because this is the point where many parents start to lose control.

What should we do when a little one throws a tantrum? There are no absolutes, but here are some ideas:

1. Don't panic; stay calm.
2. Don't yell or scream.
3. Before you do anything, say "I love you."
4. Don't give in to pressure.
5. Lead the infant to another room and say, "You can come out as soon as you calm down."

What we must avoid is giving credence to the tantrum. Initially, we might ignore the power play and this might be sufficient. If this fails, then the technique of taking him/her to another room becomes appropriate. It is important to allow the child to return as soon as the tantrum ends. This permits a choice of behavior which brings reward and prevents our need to punish.

Nose Picking, Thumb Sucking

Many children pursue these tactile-rewarding habits. These will pass as adults demonstrate more appropriate behavior; the danger is that the child will be shamed and become guilty because of the way adults respond. Substitution without shaming is the key.

"When I want to clear my nose, I use my handkerchief." The child does as is demonstrated and the adult says, "Oh, that's very good. I like the way you did that." Shaming and threats just drive the behavior underground and add the dimension of guilt.

Underlying all suggestions for rearing successful, happy children is the need to relate to others in a social environment. There is a clue here for parents: Children need to practice social skills, to learn to get along with others at the earliest age possible. This means that parents must plan for these socialization skills.

Sunday School is fine if teachers are positive. Nursery school, which allows brief periods of play with other children with the length of time gradually increasing, provides another chance for learning cooperation. Ideally, nursery school should be a happy opportunity rather than a negative solution to an economic problem brought on by parental employment.

The way parents present the nursery school experience has much to do with whether or not there will be benefit or harm from the experience. The attitudes of infants are the most malleable they will ever be in a lifetime. If children feel they are in nursery school because they are a burden, negative self-images accrue. If this image can be prevented and nursery school is a happy place, positive socially, other skills can develop. "Warehousing" of kids delivers a message that they are a bother to society; this devastates self-image and leads to anti-social behavior.

Small children also need to start learning to accept financial responsibility early in life. A small allowance for purely discretionary spending is helpful. Advice should be given so the child gets experience with saving up for larger purchases, borrowing and paying back, and also making restitution when something is broken. As the child grows, he or she will need progressively less assistance in handling discretionary funds and this allows steps toward maturity and independence. Care must always be taken not to ask more than the child is capable of mastering, but my experience shows me that there is a greater danger of expecting too little than too much.

Value systems of the home are absorbed through all of the infant's senses. When these values are consistent from day to day, great security is derived; inconsistency produces confusion and brings the child into conflict with adults in the home. The challenge for parents is clear.

As the infant grows, he or she will be more able to deal with the conflicts between the value systems of home and the rest of the world. Support will still be needed but the security

Value systems of the home are absorbed through all of the infant's senses.

base should be sufficient to sustain the growing child if early imprinting has been achieved.

"Daddy, why does Grandaddy smoke when you said it is so bad?" The home values come in conflict with outside experiences and a youngster wonders about the difference.

"That is Grandaddy's choice," replies the parent. "But in our home, we don't do that." If the values taught and lived in the home have been consistent, this is all the explanation that will be needed.

Chapter 8
Nurture the Rebelling Adolescent

"I don't know what suddenly got into her," sighs a frustrated parent. "We were always so close until suddenly, at age fourteen, she rejected me in favor of her friends."

Another parent complains, "He started acting like he did when he was two years old! When he reached sixteen I felt I was dealing with a stubborn two-year-old only now he was driving a car instead of a tricycle."

These parents are dealing with behavior that is in all probability normal, but if the parental reaction is incorrect, the normal behavior may become misbehavior. The period of adolescence is a particularly challenging time for us to pursue our three goals, and we must remind ourselves of them: that every act or decision must build the individual, build the family, and be more than fair to everyone. Just when we think parenting will be getting easier, along comes adolescence with challenges like we have never seen before.

It is dangerous to generalize too much about this period of life because no two children react exactly the same way. Even in the same child, patterns of behavior fluctuate widely and rapidly. A general guideline can be given, though, which is likely to help us meet our three goals: Show constant love but let them learn to make their own decisions.

The most empathetic adults will be those who remember these years and want to do the thing most helpful in bridging this period. It is not a time for "holier than thou" speeches about how things are easy today compared to years past.

The adolescent is preparing for adulthood by beginning to practice the things adults must do. This means a natural pulling away from parents, a practicing for independence. Some children grasp these opportunities while others try to retreat to the security of childhood. It is an uneven time at best and many parents misunderstand the movement toward independence. How much to hold on, how much to let go—this is the dilemma for the parent. Some will interpret the acts of their offspring as rejection and act accordingly. Some will find the fluctuating behavior of the adolescent so frustrating that they will isolate themselves from the child just at a time when he or she has a great need for belonging.

If adults in the environment do not respond appropriately the adolescent is adrift because other adolescents to whom he or she turns are also unstable at this time. The desire for peer acceptance is stronger during this period than at any other time. What develops is the "blind leading the blind," as young people imitate each other's behavior. I often suggest to parents that there is less risk in doing the wrong thing than in doing nothing at all. At the very least, action communicates caring; the worst fear of teenagers is to be ignored. Ideally, with some thought and guidance, parents can act in a way that communicates caring and also contributes to meeting the needs of the girl or boy.

Understand Normal Behavior

"She talks to her friends on the phone incessantly, spends hours fixing her hair, and thinks any advice I give is old-fashioned. She would rather stay home than go with the family on vacation. She used to love to go on trips with us. She doesn't even like us to go to PTA meetings to meet her

During adolescence
parents should
exercise
enough control to
give the child
security and
permit
enough freedom to
promote maturity.

teachers; in years past she begged us to go. What is wrong with her?"

Probably nothing! Adolescents do such things, and if parents are patient and avoid unnecessary confrontation, all will survive.

Project Love Even If It Is Not Returned

It is easy to misunderstand the teenagers' growing need for independence because, in youthful naivete, their attempts to stand alone can have negative results. The adolescent is not aware of his or her changing emotional needs. Parents suddenly seem old-fashioned. A show of affection toward them seems childish. In the privacy of home a touch, a hug, even though it is shrugged off, is the proper thing for parents to do. "I love you" may not be given back, but it needs to be said anyway. Don't stop loving when they seem to be rejecting is the advice I give parents. Make loving them obvious in the home and they will reflect it again as they become adults. Interruption of the expression of love on the part of both adolescents and adults during this period may never be restored. It is also important to make clear that the love given is unconditional. The young person may do something, show some behavior which the parents don't like. The parents dislike the act but always love the young person—no strings attached.

Control Anger

Anger is a destructive emotion which harms the person to whom it is directed and the person who harbors the anger. No good comes of it for anybody, yet it is the most common of emotions. When we avoid it we prevent a large number of problems in human relationships, particularly with our children. Anger is an extension or exacerbation of the problem and not any part of the solution. If we can avoid ever giving in to anger and instead discuss everything in a calm atmosphere, many problems will be averted.

Adolescents
challenge authority
as they grope for
their own rightful place
in the
decision-making process.
This is perfectly natural.

Provide Reasonable Boundaries

Adolescents challenge authority as they grope for their own rightful place in the decision-making process. Once again, this is perfectly natural. We must acknowledge their growing rights in this area without making the mistake of giving up our own rights or extending too much authority too soon. Their growing importance in the process means that adults must give weight to their opinions and extend as much freedom for self-determination as possible. Do not be misled in this matter. Teenagers need boundaries to help them decide what is right and wrong for them to do.

I have talked with many young people from all types of homes and I am thoroughly convinced that the happiest children come from homes where there is strong parent interest and guidance. Children have a right to be heard but not a right to always have their own way. The lack of maturity may cause them to make a decision which seems right at the time but which eventually causes harm.

Chapter 9
Cooperate When Schools Discipline

As loving parents we must be assured that the schools our children attend have a program of controlling misbehavior in a positive, growth-producing way. Our good efforts can be dissipated if the school is not sensitive to the impact of its discipline program and the school personnel use techniques which damage rather than build. Additionally, we should be assured that the school is consciously attempting to build responsible students through a unified program designed for that purpose.

In some areas the dunce stool and similar degrading practices are still in use. As a new school administrator in one district, I was shocked to find teachers taping kids to their desks and taping their mouths shut for punishment. My first reaction when I was told about it was disbelief, but it turned out to be true.

Please do not misunderstand what I am saying. We have an obligation to cooperate fully with schools and we should not be adversarial if this can be avoided. At the same time, we must know that the teachers who work with our kids are enlightened in the proper ways of *building* young people when they deal with them in every situation. Ideally, the home and school will work together to provide the very best discipline environment.

What should we expect from the school? Ideally, the school should be emphasizing the same goals as our program in the home, though terms may vary and techniques of implementation may differ. Whatever the system, the school should operate in a way that builds the individual, the school group, and is more than fair to everyone. The following pages outline a program which harmonizes with our goals. We must insist upon this or a similarly constructed program if we are to best meet our obligations as loving parents.

We should expect the educational program to provide a high level of excitement so that children are fully occupied with real learning activities. Under-challenged students will find activities to create excitement if these are not provided. Boring classes led by uninspired teachers create an atmosphere ripe for misbehavior.

We should also be able to expect a curriculum which builds on the strengths of learners. People grow best when their strengths are identified; highlighting weaknesses lowers self-image and rubs the sore spot so it cannot heal. Classes labeled "remedial" or "slow learner" serve as constant reminders to the students that something is wrong with them. Every child has strengths, but these may not be developed if total emphasis is upon the weaknesses.

The grouping and grading of students are closely related and both have great impact upon self-image. Grades given on assignments should communicate what was done right. It may seem insignificant, but marking ninety correct rather than ten wrong on a paper puts achievement in the spotlight rather than failure. Special care should be given to this in the early grades where self-images are still quite fragile. The child who gets a C on a report card in first grade due to lack of physical or intellectual maturity can interpret the grade as a prophecy to be lived out for a lifetime.

As parents, we should insist that schools operate according to these principles, while also preparing learners for the real world where logical consequences control behavior. We should not expect the school to loan replacements for forgotten

Boring classes
led by
uninspired teachers
create an atmosphere
ripe for
misbehavior.

pencils or lunch money and thus reinforce behavior that will not prepare the students for a successful life. Schools should not bail out kids any more than parents should. If we want a program that prepares responsible citizens then we must support treatment that produces responsibility.

I recall a father who objected vehemently to having his child pay a breakage fee in an industrial arts class. He said that his son should have to pay only if he personally broke an item. I explained to him that it is not always possible to know who broke an item. Many times the culprit isn't known and sometimes the students know who broke an item and won't tell. The father's objections were even stronger after my explanation.

I finally won him to my way of thinking when I used this analogy. Suppose someone vandalizes playground equipment in the park. The vandals aren't discovered or those who know who did it won't tell. Don't all citizens have to pay? Similarly, wasn't it a lesson in responsibility to have the students pay the fee unless they reported the culprit or the culprit truly wasn't known? The father then agreed and even went a step further and improved my analogy. He said he was going to have his son work to earn the money for the breakage fee. Now *there* is a practical lesson in becoming a responsible citizen in the real world.

It is not intended that this book give details about how the school should implement its program of positive discipline. It is well, however, for parents to have some notion about how to determine that such a program is really in place. I believe parents can recognize the steps which are inherent in all good systems of school discipline. The sequential program which follows is presented as an example of the steps in a typical program.

Step 1: Prevent

Great teaching is the best method of preventing misbehavior in the school. Instructors should be prepared, work should start immediately at the begining of class, and goals should be

*Schools should not
bail out kids . . . .
If we want a program
that prepares
responsible citizens,
then we must support
treatment that produces
responsibility.*

clearly stated. The teacher should be obviously enthusiastic about the class and subject. Work given should be appropriate to the maturity of students, challenging but not too difficult for mastery with reasonable effort. There should be no long list of don'ts which only serve to remind young people of misbehavior and establish expectations of problems.

Step 2: Ignore

Being too sensitive to minor infractions which are occasional rather than chronic can cause unnecessary confrontation. The teacher who makes a great issue out of the first instance of tardiness, particularly in front of the rest of the class, can cause emotions to flare and statements to be made which are problems larger than a simple tardy. A first tardy might simply be ignored or, if a small penalty is the policy it could be assessed privately after class. This gentle acknowledgement may be all that is needed to prevent further occurrences.

I had a student fall asleep in my class once and my first impulse was to do something right then. Fortunately, I went on with the lesson and approached the student after class. He apologized, offering a logical reason why he hadn't slept the night before, and unnecessary confrontation was avoided. He never was a problem after that. If I had come down hard the first time, I believe a larger problem may have resulted. His falling asleep did force me to reevaluate my teaching style for that lesson, however.

Step 3: Counsel

In this step we assume that the minor misbehavior has been repeated. The teacher should talk with the student to be sure that he or she understands that the behavior is causing a problem. Specific direction should be given in terms of what must be done to correct the situation. No attempt should be made by the teacher who is making the judgement and decision to elicit a promise of improvement. This implies the student has a choice. The time for discussion is over and the time for direction is at hand.

Step 4: Involve Others

The misbehavior has been repeated even after the teacher has counseled the student. It is time for the teacher to put the problem in the hands of others so that disruption to the class is minimized. The teacher has done all that can be expected in the classroom setting. Parents, the school counselor, or the administrator step in to handle the problem from this point, working together with the teacher to devise the plan. Every effort should be made to have the school authorities work with parents as colleagues rather than as adversaries.

Step 5: Use Logical Consequences

The school–and–parent team agree upon a plan of rewards or penalties which are explained until understood by the young person. The student makes the choice. When certain accomplishments are made, rewards such as recreational activities, visits with friends, movies, etc., are permitted. When obligations are not met, penalties, outlined in advance, are assessed. The parents and school monitor the program without emotion and the young person makes the choices. There is no equivocation in the assessment of penalties.

Step 6: Recognize Incremental Improvement

By the time this step is reached, the situation is serious, and much discussion has taken place with the student. There is danger that negative feelings have developed in the people involved. Care must be taken to keep these negative feelings from becoming negative expectations. Hope must not be lost. Neither should there be an expectation of instant turnaround in behavior that has reached this critical stage. Extra effort must be given to recognize any degree of improvement, because this is the direction which must be reinforced. Rather than miraculous change, we are looking for a positive trend which can be built upon for long-range growth in the right direction.

Step 7: Try Alternative Education

Movement to this step means that success has not been achieved in the previous steps; strong efforts have not worked. Despite the devotion of a great amount of parent and school personnel time, the problem behavior persists. We must face the fact that this problem cannot be solved at this time with the student remaining in the normal school setting. It is time to try a last resort effort involving an alternative school approach.

Such efforts are costly to the schools, so the alternative education which parents can reasonably expect must depend on school resources. Some techniques, such as on- campus suspension or a modified school day in which the student remains in his classes where there has *not* been a problem, are less expensive. If a separate alternative school is established, the cost for educating each child is tripled. Parents should be willing to cooperate with all reasonable attempts made by the school including paying tuition to support such special programs.

Step 8: Expel, Using Due Process

All good faith efforts have failed and the school has done everything possible to help the student rehabilitate, but the behavior is still unacceptable. It is time for the parents or another community agency to take full responsibility. This might mean a private school with a special program to deal with anti-social behavior, tutoring, or no school at all. We don't like to admit it, but there are a few cases where the school cannot permit a student to remain, out of fairness to other students.

Care must be taken to make sure that all constitutional and civil rights are accorded prior to expulsion. These safeguards are necessary to assure that fair treatment has been given at every step of the process and that the situation merits this severe final action.

It should also be pointed out that in some cases, removal may be required without going through the previously outlined steps. If there is an act of violence such as a physical attack on a teacher, the student may have to be expelled for that action alone. Schools must keep as a primary consideration the welfare of the large group of students who maintain excellent or at least reasonably good behavior.

Chapter 10
Address Special Needs of
the Gifted and Handicapped

Thus far I have been discussing topics related to the development of positive behavior in all children. Most of what I have said would be entirely applicable to children with exceptionally high intelligence and to children who have a physical or mental handicap. Indeed, gifted children and handicapped children have much in common, because either condition can make them feel different in their own minds and seem different to those around them. This conscious or unconscious judgement can cause behavior problems.

In the case of gifted or especially talented children it is important to understand that the special ability does not in any way assure good behavior any more than it assures high achievement in learning. Brightness can be channeled into high achievement, but the same fertile soil can grow weeds as well as flowers. Bright children have been known to channel their brainpower into creative misbehavior. They can also outsmart the system and use their talents to avoid learning. The highest dropout rate in one large American city school district is among seventeen-year-old gifted girls!

Handicapped children can use their condition as an excuse for not performing or behaving. The natural feeling of sympathy from others gives the youngster a chance to exploit

In the case of
gifted children,
it is important to understand
that special ability does not
in any way assure
good behavior
any more than it assures
high achievement.

the condition. The opportunity to avoid consequences or to avoid work by such exploitation is obviously tempting, but a double standard of expectations by adults can do much harm. Unnecessary sympathy is not the way to do what is best for a handicapped person; it can actually extend the handicap.

I talked earlier about the natural stereotyping and development of self-images which occur as children perceive themselves. Giftedness or handicaps must be seen in the context of the total individual. The handicap must be understood as one tiny part of the totality of the person and not as a factor greater than the myriad of capabilities. The gifted child should see the gift as one part of a totality, most of which is normal, just like everybody else. The self-image must not be unduly distorted by any condition of specialness.

Since apart from the gift or handicap this child is just like all other children, I believe the treatment given and behavior expected of the gifted/handicapped child should be as much like that of the other children as possible. A term sometimes given to the approach is "mainstreaming"—putting the gifted/handicapped person in normal situations wherever possible. The gift or handicap is not ignored but neither is it given more importance than it deserves. The following guidelines may be helpful in mainstreaming the special child and avoiding behavior problems which could arise because of the specialness.

Never Allow Giftedness or Handicaps to be Used as Excuses

Every child should be held to high standards of behavior and performance in every instance possible. The loss of a limb does not warrant failure to participate in all physical activity. It would be reasonable to expect participation in physical activities that don't require two legs or even competition against other handicapped persons. Similarly, children with Down's Syndrome should not necessarily be excused from attempting any activity in which they have the ability to compete fairly. Some physically or mentally impaired children

S*ince the*
gifted/handicapped child
is mostly like
all other children,
the treatment given and
behavior expected should
be as much like
other children as
possible.

are denied the opportunity to take part in *all* activities just because there is a handicap in *one* area. This is unfair, nongrowth producing, and a cause of misbehavior.

Gifted students are sometimes exempted from physical and social activities and channeled full time into purely intellectual pursuits. This can cause them to grow up without skills necessary to fit into society. Sooner or later they will have to succeed in a social world, one which does not excuse their behavior just because they are gifted. Special talent must never be allowed to excuse children from cooperating with other children as equals when rights or obligations are being considered.

Emphasize Success in the Real World

The behaviors we want children to learn are those which bring success in the real world. This was discussed at length in a previous chapter, but it must be particularly emphasized here in its application to gifted and handicapped children. The child must learn not to exploit the feelings of sympathy toward handicapped people, because in the long run this fails to build skills for life. Neither should intellectual advantages be mistaken for accomplishment; the smart person must still get an education or brainpower is wasted. Both the gifted and handicapped must assess their individual situations and decide how to succeed in a world where they will be different from the majority of people.

Stress Service to Others

It is unhealthy for any individual to turn completely inward in his or her thinking. This can happen to handicapped or gifted persons because they are different from other people. The gifted can become arrogant and overbearing rather than the leaders they could be. The handicapped can withdraw into self-pity. These conditions cause eccentricities at best and severely disturbed behavior at worst.

A good way to avoid this is to teach them while they are young to serve others. Not only does this prevent inward thinking such as self-pity, but it gives an enhanced feeling of self-worth. The good feeling of service satisfies ego needs and promotes social skills. Rather than an outcast, the special young person becomes a valuable, functioning member of society.

Chapter 11
Confront Drug Problems with Firmness

It always amazes me when some person tries to give a simple explanation of why alcohol and other drugs have become such a problem in America and around the world. Often a single cause is cited as "the" reason this horrible problem has reached epidemic proportions. This is simply naive. There are many diverse causes: psychological, sociological, economic, and cultural.

Though the causes are complicated, that is no reason to assume that prevention and cure need to be complicated. My recommendation for dealing with the problem will be simple but effective because the approaches which I have seen work are simple enough to be understood and put into use by anyone. I have also seen failure when drug programs become unduly complicated, esoteric, and philosophical.

A look at some recent history may be helpful to put the issue in perspective, though no attempt is made to examine why these events occurred. The once strong family unit has given way to loosely structured homes where parental control has been diminished. Greater freedom at a young age challenges young people to make decisions beyond their maturity. School dropouts cannot find jobs as they once did, so they are available and vulnerable to drugs as a means of escape and employment as they distribute these substances to peers. The crowding together of people into urban areas as opposed to the distances characteristic of agrarian society exacerbates the problem. The young person who does poorly in school or who drops out has low self-esteem and becomes an easy target for anything that promises relief. As the demand for drugs increases, the availability widens, so it is not uncommon to find drugs in colleges, high schools, and even in elementary schools.

Whether or not we applaud or deplore this age of freedom makes little difference. It is a reality and it has permitted drug abuse to flourish. Loving parents must intervene firmly, lest the behavior become harmful to the individual, the family, and society as a whole. Throughout this book I have recommended parental restraint, allowing logical consequences to teach the lesson. In this instance, I will depart from that stance because to wait for the consequences to teach the lesson may be life-threatening. Parents must do at least the following things to meet their obligations.

Admit the Potential Danger

"I don't know how I could have been so blind," admitted the distraught parent. "The signs were everywhere. His grades had fallen, he was running with the wrong crowd, and our conversations were really fights. Still, it was a shocker when the police called me to say he was picked up for drunken driving in a stolen car."

Some parents can't bring themselves to the realization that drug problems can occur in any family. It's like having an accident: It is the kind of thing that only happens to other people. The truth is it can happen to anyone, in any school or community, and in any economic group. This recognition of the reality and universal nature of the threat is the first step in prevention—the thing that makes us realistically on our guard. It doesn't mean that we are fatalistic in our thinking or down on kids. It does recognize that all children, not just "bad" children, are vulnerable given a certain set of circumstances. It also recognizes that we are not necessarily bad parents if a

As the demand for
drugs increases,
the availability widens,
so it is not uncommon
to find drugs in colleges,
high schools,
and even elementary
schools.

problem arises. Even the best prevention is sometimes inadequate.

It is a mistake to believe that a child is too young to experiment with drugs. There are critical periods such as adolescence when experimentation is statistically very high but problems sometimes arise in six- and seven-year-olds, especially with alcohol. While I was a school administrator, an eleven-year-old died at a birthday party from overdosing on prescription pills he had taken from the home medicine cabinet. His friends said he had gotten the idea from a television movie he had seen. As a farm boy, I was encouraged by older boys when I was seven to get high by smelling the gasoline tank on our tractor. Fortunately for me, my father caught me and applied the proper measure to correct my behavior. Kids see parents take a pill to feel good; isn't it logical they could do the same? The threat of drugs is everywhere in many forms.

Understand Causes and Prevention

Curiosity and the urge to experiment are natural in boys and girls. However, if the danger has been made known, it is not natural for them to feel they must try drugs; they do not have to be hit by a car to be taught to stay out of the street. What I am saying is that when young people use drugs in spite of what they know about the dangers, there is a cause greater than normal curiosity.

Often the same things which lead to other forms of antisocial behavior also cause drug problems. If the child has low self-esteem and does not get recognition in socially acceptable ways such as good grades, attention or escape is sought to fill the void. If there is a feeling of being unimportant or unloved, drugs can be the refuge. Such insecure children are also very susceptible to peer pressure.

Children who feel good about themselves, who experience success in school, and who enjoy family relationships have no need for drugs. These, then, must be our goals to foster a situation which creates immunity to the disease. Many

Some parents can't bring themselves to the realization that drug problems can occur in any family.

techniques have been explored in previous chapters to help parents achieve these goals, and there are other books devoted to positive parenting. What children need is structure and boundaries from the beginning of life so they are never in a quandary as to what behavior is appropriate for themselves.

Educate the Child

Parents are often reluctant to teach about dangers such as drugs, fearing this might put ideas into kid's heads. This is much like the Victorian idea about sex education: Don't teach them, because if they don't know about sex they won't be interested. Young people will learn about drugs somewhere; it is best they learn the truth from someone who has their best interests at heart.

The facts should be taught appropriately to the age of the learner. This education should be routine so as not to glamorize the problem. Parents who don't have the facts themselves must first learn them, because no other person or agency can be relied upon to do the job. Schools and churches cannot fill the parents' role adequately and besides, most efforts by such institutions are usually too late, designed more to rehabilitate than prevent.

Be Alert to the Presence of Drugs

I firmly believe that children should have as much privacy as possible while they are growing up. They need to have a haven where they have ownership of their space. This does not mean that parents are banned from the room. Mother and Dad should be in the room for short periods on a daily basis. This leaves plenty of time for privacy. Parents do not go there to snoop, but their eyes are open to signs of potential trouble. It amazes me to read in the newspaper that a young person had drugs or a gun in his or her bedroom and the parents didn't know it. Our parenting must involve closer contacts than such a situation reveals.

If we have questions about what a child is doing in the room, as elsewhere, we seek answers, because this is what loving parents do. Our response to reluctance on the part of the child is that our love for them demands we check to see that their best interests are being served. When something seems to be wrong, we must find out what and why.

When grades drop, attitudes change, or the child shows any other problem sign, we get to the bottom of it before the situation becomes severe. Praying is fine, but not enough. Our prayers that all is well or that this is a minor, temporary problem must be accompanied by our action. If a problem exists, prompt action may prevent a more severe problem later.

Set a Good Example

Charlie was a Little League coach, although not the wholesome type that I think is more typical. I saw him try to live out his own sports career frustrations through his son, who was a member of the team he coached. He taught his team how to win at any cost, how to bend the rules, and how to cheat if necessary for a victory. He had lost sight of the true purposes of competition. I also remember how Charlie cried in my office one day when he learned his son was being disqualified from high school competition because he had taken drugs before a high school game.

Values and self-control systems must be built into young people at an early age. Much of this comes from emulation of adults the child is exposed to in the home and community at large. The parental example of self-control is a primary one. The mother or father who abuses alcohol or other drugs, even occasionally, is making a strong statement that this kind of behavior is all right.

Cooperate with Schools and Other Agencies

The problem of drug abuse is pervasive enough to challenge the best efforts of all of us. Still, I find much energy dissipated in intramural struggles between people. Let's get together and work as a team. Let's cooperate with the school, for example. If a child has a problem which is discovered at school, our first impulse should be to work with the teachers rather than become defensive. Some parents immediately hire a lawyer to get out of the present predicament with the least penalty. This example for the child can be the very attitude and approach which permits a much more difficult problem to occur later.

Chapter 12
Use Physical Punishment Sparingly

I guess there will always be a great difference of opinion as to whether or not physical punishment should ever be used. My judgement is that it is appropriate and advisable in certain situations at specific ages. The word *punishment* itself is one that I avoid but in this case I am using *punishment* as a logical consequence for misbehavior of young children.

Spanking should be used between the ages of two and six. It provides a logical consequence for misbehavior that is easily understood by the child and it wipes the slate clean very quickly so the infant can be restored to grace without waiting a long time. Shaming or other psychological punishments are dangerous during this delicate period when self-images are being developed.

My fear in recommending corporal punishment is that parents will abuse the technique. I implore all adults to adhere strictly to the guidelines which I lay down for any use of physical punishment. It is easy for a big person to go too far with a relatively tender little person. Most physical punishment I have viewed has violated the rules I suggest. In honesty, I must admit that as a parent I did not always follow them fully. When I did, I think I did some of my best parenting, but it wasn't easy to do it right.

My children are grown and now I have grandchildren, but I vividly recall what it was like to face the awesome task of spanking a five-year-old who has tested your patience. You love the kid more than anything on earth but you don't like him or her right now and you're angry at yourself for being angry. How grateful I was later when I remembered to count to ten before I acted.

When I did it right, the ritual went something like this: As soon as the infraction occured, I took my child into a bedroom away from playmates or other family members. I explained that I loved him or her and because of this I had to do what loving parents did. A gentle spanking was administered on the buttocks and then I wiped the tears, we hugged and went back out into society. If they only knew how hard it was to give those swats!

In retrospect, I think the procedure I have just described is pretty close to the ideal. My grown children seem to agree as they look back on the situation. This reinforcement by my own children and the research I have done in the intervening years cause me to suggest the following strict rules for physical punishment.

Only When They Are Small

Using physical punishment after the age of six is demeaning to the child and unnecessary. Older children are capable of reasoning at a sophisticated level and continuing to spank denies that reasoning skills have been achieved. Additionally, the older child has freedom which can be restricted as a logical consequence or rewards which can be withheld. While negating the need for physical punishment, the use of logical consequences makes a statement which recognizes the growing maturity and establishes expectations or goals which are healthy.

Never in Anger

Physical punishment done in anger will probably 1) be too severe, 2) lack any growth-producing quality, and 3) provide

Physical punishment done
in anger will probably

1.

be too severe,

2.

lack any growth-producing
quality, and

3.

provide a source of regret
for a long time to come.

a source of regret for a long time to come. The following illustrates these truths.

I came home from work one evening to find my six-year-old son writing on his toy blackboard with a new piece of chalk. Beside him was a whole box of chalk which neither his mother nor I had bought. I immediately assumed he had stolen it from school. With obvious suspicion in my voice I asked him where he had gotten the chalk.

He told me that a neighbor had dropped it in the gutter and then told him he could have it all. I wasn't about to fall for such a wildly obvious lie. I grabbed him (too hard) by the arm to take him to face the neighbor who had allegedly given the chalk.

To my shocked surprise, the neighbor gave this explanation:

"I was in a hurry to get to school when a whole box of chalk [she used it in her work] fell into the gutter. Rather than stop to get it, I told your son he could have it."

It was exactly the way he told me! He accepted my repeated apologies and the bruises on his arms have long since healed. The bruises on my heart remain.

Indignity, Not Pain

The purpose of spanking is not to hurt the child, but to communicate with someone at an age when this is the best form of communication. The punishment is unpleasant to the child; this is necessary to provide the negative consequence. But the unpleasantness should come more from the indignity which is experienced than from physical pain. You don't have to hurt to correct and increasing the hurt does not increase the effectiveness of the punishment.

Never in Public

The indignity of having a parent disappointed enough to spank is sufficient. No one else should observe the spanking. A public punishment will distract the child or cause him or her to have to do something to save face. If spanking is necessary when others are present, such as in a car, only one adult punishes. All others must stay out of the situation.

Only with the Hand

Paddles, straps, or switches are unnecessary and detrimental. The fact that such are held at the ready anticipates there will be a problem and assumes the worst. When paddling becomes necessary, the hand is sufficient to administer correction and decreases the possibility of abuse.

Only on the Bottom

The muscles of the buttocks are ideally suited for absorbing enough communication to get a child's attention without a high risk of physical harm. There is absolutely no justification ever, under any circumstances, to strike a child anywhere but the rear end. If a parent slaps a child's face, it is likely the slap was in anger. As far as I am concerned, a slap in the face or anywhere but the buttocks is a form of assault.

If You Leave a Mark, Seek Help

Child abuse is a serious problem in the United States and around the world. The typical abuser is not a vicious person who does this out of intent. Generally, it is a person who loves the abused child but loses control occasionally or frequently. If, after paddling your child, you feel you were venting anger or if you feel you struck too hard, *cease using all physical punishment.* If you ever notice a mark (bruise, swelling, etc.), cease physical punishment and seek the help of a counselor, the local mental health representatives, or a member of the clergy. If you left a mark, something is wrong!

Y*ou don't have to hurt to correct and increasing the hurt does not increase the effectiveness of the punishment.*

Chapter 13
Teach Personal Organization

After years of teaching and administering public schools I can tell you that intelligence is not enough to bring success in school or life. Children with similar abilities often succeed or fail because of attitudes toward their work and their ability to focus efforts through good personal organization. The difference in achievement between equally talented children can be amazing. The following examples are actually composite characterizations of many boys and girls I have known.

Jerry meant well but it seemed he could never meet his obligations. Repeated tardiness kept him in hot water and on the bad side of teachers. His grades were lowered, not because of the quality of work, but because assignments were usually turned in late. He forgot his gym suit, pencils, and books. His parents said he would forget his head if it were not attached to him. At home and school he started many tasks but finished few. Other students didn't want to work with him because he let the team down. This bright boy made marginal grades due almost entirely to lack of organization and self-discipline.

Michael was also bright, but to this dimension of high intelligence he also added a high degree of personal organization. He was not compulsive with his tasks, indeed quite the opposite. The simple techniques of planning he used prevented the need for compulsiveness or rushing in his work. Teachers bragged of his conscientiousness and, I am sure, added points to his grades for pleasing them. He suffered no penalties for tardiness, but instead got extra credit for being early. At home he planned his work and worked his plan, thus adding to his productivity and favor with his parents.

Many behavior problems would be prevented if a young person followed Michael's example. As loving parents we must help our children to develop these winning habits so that achievement is accelerated and problems are diminished. This will not occur by chance; the skills of good personal organization must be taught. The following checklist can serve as a guide.

Goal-Setting and Planning

A straight line is always the shortest distance to achievement whether it be the completion of a task or the realization of ambition. Poor goal-setting extends the time necessary for achievement or results in non-achievement. For example, some college students graduate with the exact minimum of credits necessary while others take many additional hours as they move aimlessly toward vague goals.

The concept of goals is absorbed at a very early age and becomes a symptom of a success-oriented attitude. If we ask kindergarten-age children what they want to be when they grow up, many have an idea—some won't. It is true that few will still have the same career goal later in life, but those with a concept of goals tend to be more successful at all ages. The knowledge that today's work builds toward something later increases the importance of the work and intensifies effort.

When we approach a task, we must share with children the goal we are attempting to achieve so that they imitate the logic.

Before we start, we picture the end result and the sequence of steps between our present position and the conclusion. When children help mom and dad make a garden, build a doghouse, or even a model out of blocks, they first discuss: What will it be like when it is finished? What do we do first? What will be the next step? This kind of discussion builds into the child's mind how goals are set and demonstrates their importance to success.

We can also teach how planning and goal-setting prevent crises in our life. If a term paper is due in six weeks, many students start on it a few days before it is due and experience pressure to get it done on time. They burn the midnight oil and often turn in work which is not as well done as it could be. With planning, this or any other job can be broken down into steps and a portion done each week so that the paper is done without last-minute rushing. There is time to review the work and insure that it is the very best quality possible. An explanation of the effect of planning will make sense, and, if modeled by the one giving the advice, will likely be adopted.

Write It Down

Someone once observed, "One dull pencil is better than two sharp minds when it comes to remembering." This sounds a bit silly, but it is very true that the good habit of making a list prevents forgetting and the penalties which result. We must teach our children to make simple to-do lists and to carry a notepad to write down things such as homework assignments which must be remembered.

It is also important to have a checklist to go over prior to leaving home in the morning so nothing is forgotten. Then a separate list is made of things which must be done that day. This gives a feeling of confidence and helps overcome procrastination. The same list which gives such momentum in the morning also gives a feeling of accomplishment at the end of the day when the list has lines drawn through each of the items.

A *straight line
is always the
shortest distance to
achievement
whether it be the
completion of a task or the
realization of ambition.*

One Thing at a Time

Young people must be taught to value work completed rather than jobs started. The way to get the most done is to concentrate firmly on one task until it is done before starting another. When I talk with young people about homework, I tell them to do the hardest subject first, to completion, and then do the next hardest until everything is finished. Such a simple idea, but in reality a simply profound idea.

Work According to Priorities

The tendency for young people is to work on what is most interesting or closest at hand. When you think of it, maturity is really the disciplining of oneself to do what is most important when we would rather do something else. We must teach young people to ask themselves, "What is really most important for me to do right now in terms of my chosen goals?" This will enable them to make good choices which bring long-term happiness, not just short-term pleasure.

Self-Reward

Another concept that pays off in terms of successful life skills is to build into our schedules a payoff for conscientious effort. This intensifies our efforts and gives us something to anticipate with pleasure. For example, "When I finish this chore, I will sit down and read something just for fun." This attitude makes the work more palatable and also enhances the joy of the reward. Done in reverse, there is a reverse effect; if I rest and then work, there is nothing pleasant to anticipate so the work seems harder.

Schedule Relaxation

All through this chapter I have been attempting to suggest a comfortably organized lifestyle which balances work and play. If we can really teach our children the importance of this we will make them more successful, we will prevent many problems which could cause them difficulty, and we will help

Young people
must be taught
to value
work completed
rather than jobs
started.

them enjoy life. The danger when teaching personal organization is that it will be interpreted that work alone is important. It must be stressed that a balance is the goal.

The best way is to instruct and show by our example that work and rest both must be scheduled. The reason is simple: both are important. There is enough time in life for everything we really have to do, including getting the proper rest to keep our energies high and our stress down. Good personal organization makes possible the well-balanced life.

Chapter 14
Give Special Care in
One-Parent Homes

Ethel Brant (not her real name) was a member of the PTA in a school where I was principal. I noticed her in particular at the meeting of parents before school started; she stood out because she was the only one who brought her eleven-year-old child along to the meeting and she was so intense in her demeanor. Her questions revealed an insecurity, an expectation that the school might not be properly controlled. Little did I know this was only the beginning; I would get to know Edward and his mother very well that year.

Mrs. Brant's calls to my office were frequent. Someone was always picking on Edward or the school was not doing enough for him. Edward's school records bulged with anecdotal incidents entered by teachers, and the child seemed to have been tested by every psychologist in the city. Edward had tantrums in class, lost bladder and bowel control at times, and was the brunt of every cruel trick by classmates. What a sad, almost hopeless, situation had evolved in this home in the seven years since Mrs. Brant's divorce.

The causes of this depressing situation were obvious. This woman had warped her son's personality by being severely overprotective. The condition had grown worse year by year as the overprotection rendered Edward less capable of coping,

The probability of smothering overprotection and other parent-child problems is much greater when one parent has the total childrearing responsibility.

which, in turn, resulted in even greater overprotection.

I do not imply that this is typical of a one-parent home, nor that a divorced person is likely to react with such severe overprotection of a child or children. My purpose is to demonstrate a possible negative situation which can develop. Indeed, this could even develop in a two-parent home, but is less likely. The incidence of smothering overprotection and other parent-child problems is much greater when one parent has the total childrearing responsibility.

If one faces the responsibility of raising a child by oneself, there are certain guidelines to follow in preventing self-destructive behavior in the child. It is also important to try to compensate to some degree for the missing parent. The challenge is to provide a home environment which is as effective as a fine two-parent home. This is difficult but not impossible.

The remaining parent must do as much as he or she can to fill any void by playing both parental roles. Anything less shortchanges the child. This double duty is taxing compared to shared responsibility but I have seen it done well. I remember a mother who coached a Little League team for her son while earning a living, caring for the home, and accomplishing everything else that a father and mother would have done. She planned well, worked hard, and succeeded because she understood and accepted the challenges.

It is important to expose the child to strong examples which compensate for the missing mate. Spending time with two-parent families such as relatives, or with friends on vacation can be helpful. Role models are powerful with young children, so wise choices must be made in choosing contacts. At the same time, the child must be allowed to be with adults apart from the parent. Two weeks away at camp may be hard for the parent to accept, but it is important. The parent who has already experienced loss will have to fight extra hard the feeling of never wanting the child out of his or her sight.

In summary, the lone parent must accept the reality of the situation and plan to deal with it positively. The past cannot be

Role models are powerful with young children, so wise choices must be made in choosing contacts.

changed but the future is ours to control. The remaining parent must determine what a loving two-parent home would provide for the children and these experiences must be provided to the greatest extent possible. Extra care must be taken to help the child understand what has happened and that it is not the fault of the child. It must also be made clear that he or she will not be shortchanged in life because of the situation. The parent and child or children team up to meet the challenge and turn lemons into lemonade.

Chapter 15
Operate the Family as a Team

The emotional environment in the home both reflects and molds the behavior of all family members, especially the children. The cooperative atmosphere where all relish the success of each other and selfish feelings are controlled provides a workshop where positive life skills are practiced and learned. An environment where self-interests take priority over family interests produces spoiled children, which really means insecure children. If the atmosphere goes beyond simple selfishness to a traumatic situation, such as that produced by uncontrolled alcoholic parents, severe deviant behavior can result. I think the best way to describe the wholesome environment we seek is to work toward the family's operating as a team.

Please do not misunderstand what I am trying to suggest. The family working as a team does not imply equality of family members in terms of authority. It is imperative that relative roles of family members be spelled out so there is no confusion. The parents retain the right and obligation of making final decisions. Children must be given a forum for expression and participation commensurate with their maturity, but parents exercise final control unequivocally. There is great danger in implying that children have equal say in decision-making because there is disappointment when parents inevitably have to overrule them in some instances. Parents retain veto power; children are guaranteed participation only in the process of deciding.

This is in no way a denial of the importance of children. The involvement increases as the child grows, thus recognizing maturity. Indeed, when children are given adult responsibility too soon, they are denied childhood. It is sad when a child has been asked to step in and make adult decisions at a young age, only to be admonished later for resisting authority. An example would be street children who learn to survive on the streets and then later are punished because their survival instincts bring them into conflict with society's rules for behavior.

Neither do I imply that parents become benevolent despots. The parental role which retains final say is a loving role which permits a great deal of freedom. Neither do parents make unnecessary sacrifices to accommodate the whims of children. The best way to encourage offspring to have wholesome self-respect is to model this self-respect. The family members have equal importance even though roles differ at times, based on maturity.

The idea of royalty is repugnant to me but I am impressed with the way the British royal family gradually prepares its children to assume leadership roles. At the time of birth the child is recognized as a full family member and as a future leader, but a special period of preparation is required before the newcomer exercises any authority. The child gains power slowly in anticipation of leadership roles to follow; experiences are given to provide practice for future obligations. The sense of functioning as a team is strong at all times, no matter the roles assigned at any given stage.

The royal children are not coddled, but instead subjected to rigorous training. They go to tough schools where they are expected to achieve high marks just as do the other students. They play sports on equal terms with non-royal students. They serve their term in military branches and assume their share of public service. After they have paid their dues and demonstrated their ability, only then are they placed into positions of leadership. Their role on the team is changed to reflect the status that has been earned.

This conceptual model, while not directly applicable to our family team, does have many elements which can be used as examples of the outcomes we seek. In our situation, the maturing young person develops skills over time, ultimately reaching a point where he or she is ready to take charge of his or her individual life—or to head a new family, a new team.

Let me describe some of the situations that confront families and then illustrate how the team concept might function in these situations.

Goal-Setting

There is much talk in the business world today about the importance of synergy in maximizing the efforts of people in an organization as that group reaches toward a goal. The more the goals of individuals harmonize with company goals, the greater the level of achievement by the group and individuals. When the goals of individuals are not in harmony with the company or between individuals, energy is dissipated, less is achieved. The same is true in the family.

The family team achieves greater group and individual success by meeting and discussing what each is attempting to do and how these desired outcomes might impact on the family as a whole and upon each other. These discussions promote understanding and reduce conflict. The sessions can also be highly motivational as family members come to support each other's goals. Involvement also brings commitment through understanding how each person is an important factor in achieving family goals. There is less chance that children will feel left out at any age when they are involved to the extent that they understand and contribute.

For example, father brings up in a family discussion the fact that the interior of the house will need painting soon. Should this be done on weekends or should a week of next

It is sad when a child has been asked to step in and make adult decisions, only to be admonished later for resisting authority.

There is never enough money to fill everybody's needs and wants. Compromise and sacrifice are essential if team harmony is to be maintained.

summer's vacation be used? What colors should be used in each room? What preparations will be necessary in advance? Who will do what? As the discussion goes forth, the needs of each family member are considered and a mutually agreeable plan is adopted. What could be drudgery becomes an exciting project which is anticipated rather than dreaded. This concept works equally well in selecting such important goals as family values.

Chores

The family discussion identifies chores which are essential to the smooth functioning of the family. Individuals see how these chores contribute to the overall success of the group. The fairness of assignments is considered so that no one feels abused. Once again, a situation that could be negative turns positive and becomes a team effort with all participants feeling important and needed.

Use of Resources

Nothing has more potential for creating conflict and misunderstanding in the home than how the money is to be spent. Problems between parents and children occur because there is never enough money to fill everybody's needs and wants. Compromise and sacrifice is essential if team harmony is to be maintained.

Often children do not understand and appreciate the demands upon family income. Neither do they realize the long-term negative effect of debt which assuages a current urge to buy something. Appreciation of such factors can be achieved if the family works together to allocate financial and other resources. Complete agreement on expenditures may not always be possible but disagreement with something that is understood is far healthier than ignorance of why a decision is made. My experience shows me that open discussion in most cases does result in understanding and acceptance when decisions are fairly made and all family members participate.

Special Events

Birthdays, holidays, vacations, and similar special events are more fun when they are planned by a group such as a family group. The anticipation can be as much or more fun than the event itself. This is an excellent place to have the family generate group excitement as the members function as a team.

When my children were small we had an annual event at our church known as Advent Workshop. Families came together for an evening to make decorations for Christmas. Some of the decorations made by tiny hands were a bit crude, but the sense of making something to be enjoyed by the whole family was so exciting it is hard to describe. There are few family memories as cherished as those of the evenings we spent working together at the Advent Workshop.

Challenges

No family will escape challenges such as illness, failure, and special problems that arise in lives of individuals in the family. This is a time when the team pulls together to help the one who is experiencing the challenge. What a comfort to know that if you have a sudden special need your team will rally to your aid. This knowledge holds people together in spite of physical separation. My family is spread out over a large geographical area now that the children are grown, but I know that if I get into serious difficulty today, our three children will join my wife at my side. The team is still together sharing each other's victories and defeats.

In Summary

The concept of team that best fits the family is that in which parents play the dual role of player-coach. Mother and father are members of the team, but also are the teachers and final decision-makers. Children practice the skills assigned and grow up and, one by one, leave home. The team then has to restructure to meet changing goals. Ultimately the parents are left alone as the grown children become heads of new families. This can be a trying time because some parents feel the team is breaking up. Some will even try to set values and standards for the newly formed families and conflict occurs, especially when grandchildren come into the picture.

It is imperative for parents to let go so their children can form their own teams with their own particular goals and values. Grandparents may not always concur with the way grandchildren are being reared but no good comes from interfering. We must do the best job we can as parents and then hope and pray our children will do the same with their own.

Addendum:
Questions Parents Ask

A Collection of Questions Frequently Asked
at Dr. Fitzwater's Lectures

Q **Is there any way that parents can be assured they are doing the right things to discipline their children? We read the books on childrearing and we try hard but often have the feeling we fell short and didn't do the best we could.**

A Your feelings are natural and shared by all conscientious parents. You will not do the right or best thing every time; nobody does. The important thing is that you are trying. My advice is to keep trying but relax as you do it and don't feel you failed just because you aren't perfect. Besides, there are many ways to raise children—not just a single, best way. Loving parents keep growing just as their children do.

Q **What is the best way to handle a two-year-old who is having a tantrum?**

A The first thing that is needed is a cooling off period. Have the child go to another room until he or she can get control. Then it is permissible to return. It is very important that the child be allowed to return as soon as control is achieved. This reinforces the kind of behavior that is desired.

Q   Our three-year-old is aggressive with other children. He grabs things from them and occasionally hits them. What can we do?

A   Gently restrain him but don't admonish too severely. There is a danger that the natural assertiveness can be educated out and this would not be healthy. After restraining, demonstrate the fun of sharing and praise when the sharing is done. This may have to be repeated many times before change occurs.

Q   Our child refuses to eat and we find ourselves begging, then threatening, and often losing the confrontation.

A   Put the food out for a reasonable time. When others finish eating, take the food away without confrontation. If the food is not eaten, deny dessert or snacks until the next meal. Incidentally, an occasional missed meal is not a life-threatening event.

Q   What do you do when children lie?

A   Make them face up to the truth, but don't damage self-image by telling them they are bad. Praise them when they correct the situation, and model the importance of truthfulness.

Q   We are afraid our son is stealing money from our purse and wallet. How can we deal with this?

A   Stealing, if an isolated instance, can be corrected by having the child return what is stolen and then instructing him or her about why this is wrong. Repeated stealing may come from a feeling of insecurity. Try heaping on love, and keep listening for the possible cause of the insecurity. If the problem continues, professional help may be necessary.

Q   We don't want our boy to smoke, but we know it is still happening. What can we do?

A   Model by not smoking or if you do smoke, acknowledge your weakness and urge him to rise above your failing. Stress the health advantages of not smoking but don't preach. Often this type of behavior is encouraged by peer pressure. It is done in order to be a part of the gang. Monitor his friends and do things to build his self-image.

Q   Our nine-year-old was caught striking our dog, whom he loves. We were shocked by his behavior. What should we have done?

A   First of all, protect the animal from any abuse, whatever it takes. Get the boy to understand that animals have feelings, just like people. Counsel with him and listen for the cause of the misbehavior. Was he jealous? Did someone treat *him* that way? If it was an act of anger or a one-time event, praise his responsible acts in caring for the dog and gently remind him of the relative helplessness of the animal. Show him how animals enjoy being loved and how they return the love with loyalty.

Q   My junior-high-age child says he never has any homework and never brings books home. His teachers say he is not completing his work in school. What am I to do?

A   Let's start first with what appear to be the facts. You have determined that there is homework to be done but your son denies this, or possibly believes there is nothing to do when in reality there is. Poor schoolwork habits lead to poor performance in school and lack of satisfaction which makes schoolwork less attractive to the child. This cycle of defeat needs to be broken. Good performance leads to satisfaction and this is the direction we must go.

Determine whether your child is properly placed in school—section, grade level, etc. Try to determine if there are other factors that are making school an unpleasant experience. After these are ruled out, work with your son to set up a success mode. Require homework assignments to be written down in a special section of his notebook. You may be able to get the teachers to initial these for completeness. Set up homework hours and check on productivity. Communicate often with the teachers to assure that progress is being made. Withdraw from your monitoring role as your son shows self-discipline. Praise as warranted but stick consistently to the standards.

Q   My daughter wants to start dating; however, we feel she is still very young. How can we postpone this without causing a great deal of turmoil?

A   The desire to date is greatly fostered by our society which glamorizes dating in the media and advertising. You will also find younger children in a family more anxious to date because of the tendency to emulate older siblings. There is really nothing wrong with dating if the child is healthy emotionally and the date is appropriate to the maturity of the younger people. Ten, eleven, and twelve-year-olds occasionally going to a movie, transported by parents, is fine. Meeting at a school-chaperoned dance is also appropriate. Parents must firmly apply common sense and not be intimidated by the child or a less responsible parent. A twelve-year-old going out in a car with a sixteen-year-old is not acceptable. Very late hours and vague statements of where the children are going are also not acceptable. Parents must know where the children are going, with whom, how they will get there, and when they will be home. Give your child as much trust as possible and show faith. If your faith is violated, assess a reasonable penalty. Set your standards based on love and common sense and enforce them. The payoff will be appreciation by your children later.

Q   My husband died recently. My high-school-age son says he can't go on without his dad's support. Every day when I wake him up for school, his allergies are so bad he can't breathe. He has missed almost the whole six weeks and is failing all of his courses. What can I do?

A   This situation requires immediate attention. I suggest you get help from a professional who is qualified to counsel you and your son. Your local Medical Society or Psychological Association can recommend someone. Don't panic, but act *now*. The combination of physical symptoms and mental depression requires the skills of a professional.

Q   How do you allay the competitive and approval-seeking anxieties of a child who has no athletic ability?

A   No athletic ability? I doubt that. All people can do something well. Find out what your child likes to do and what he/she can do well, whether athletic or whatever. Show your approval and develop the strengths. This praise and approval should reduce the anxieties.

Q   My daughter is ten years old and sucks her thumb when tired or troubled. My husband and I have tried everything from putting hot sauce on it, reminding her not to, having a dentist put a cage at the roof of her mouth, and taping it. Nothing works. What can we do or should we ignore it?

A   When tired or troubled most of us do something (twist eyebrows, pull ears, bite nails) to relieve the tension. I would not worry too much about this and certainly don't scold or do something to cause even greater tension. The causes you cite are worry and fatigue. See to it that she gets adequate rest by having routines comfortably scheduled. Talk with her frequently, particularly at bedtime to let her give vent to her feelings. As she becomes more secure, the thumb sucking should cease. She is old enough to understand this reasoning herself. Talking about this with her in a positive way would not cause more tension. Tell her frequently that you love her.

Q   I can no longer communicate with my fifteen-year-old daughter. Every time I try to talk to her about anything, it results in an argument. If I ask her to wash the dishes, she feels that I am imposing on her. We have reached the point where there is a total lack of communication. What can I do?

A   Ask her once to do the dishes and never repeat yourself. Let the stack of dishes grow until she acts. If you run out of dishes, get paper plates. I think she will do the dishes eventualy, but more importantly you will deny her the fight she relishes. Your question cites lack of communication. Whenever this is a problem (and it is usually a symptom of many problems) the best way to begin to solve it is by listening. Simply indicate to her you want to hear what she has to say and then do nothing but listen and show interest. Communication should begin to improve and other problems surface where they can be addressed. When we *talk*, others formulate retorts, justifications, and rebuttal. When we *listen,* others have catharsis, become quieter, have more sympathy, and eventually they start to listen. Try it and see if it isn't better than what is happening now.

Q   I have a junior-high child who has become withdrawn. He has a very high IQ but is failing in his schoolwork and is progressively becoming a discipline problem. He was recently kicked off the

school bus and can no longer ride it to school. Eight months ago, none of this was the case. This has happened since his father left on a military tour in Germany. What can I do?

A   If this suddenly began after his father's departure, the two events are probably linked. Reassure him that the separation is temporary and encourage much communication between the two. The problem may go deeper and only rose to the surface since the authority figure is absent. No matter what, you have to handle the situation *now*. Communicate your love but help him structure for success. Reward good behavior but have reasonable consequences for misbehavior. Apply the rules consistently without exception. Don't be too quick to bail him out when he gets into trouble. Talk with his teachers and support their efforts. The home/school team is necessary here.

Q   My daughter eats every thirty or forty minutes. She makes a trail to the refrigerator and eats continuously and continues to put on weight. How can I encourage my teenager to lose weight?

A   Compulsive eating is usually caused by an underlying problem. It is a symptom, rather than a cause. Is your daughter unhappy? If so, why? Poor self-image can cause overeating, which leads to obesity, which leads to a poorer self-image. A program must be undertaken to make her feel better about herself. Don't nag; this makes it worse. Talk, listen a lot, and help her achieve success. Serve foods which help with weight control but don't confuse symptoms with cause.

Q   I am divorced and my child is having difficulty with her class assignments. I have been asked to attend a parent conference. Should I allow my ex-husband to attend since he is aware of the problem and has our daughter on the weekends? Our daughter is in the fifth grade.

A   It depends entirely on what would happen if he attended. How well do the two of you communicate? Have past differences been accommodated? Is the child being used as a pawn by either or both of you? Unless this is an unusually harmonious divorce, I think you, the parent with custody, had better go alone. Talk with your ex-husband afterward and seek his support for whatever is decided. Try every way possible to keep the child separate from your adult differences; don't let her get caught in the middle. The child of divorce still needs support and approval from both parents, but a school conference is not the place to demonstrate this unless meetings of the three of you are routine, pleasant, and frequent occurrences.

Q   My four-year-old son is unhappy in his day care. I do not want to remove him from the school simply because he is unhappy. I don't want him to think getting out of school is that easily done. However, I also don't want his first school experience to be an unhappy one. What steps can I take to make day care more pleasant for him?

A   Having a young child away from home is a special challenge for parents. If at all possible, I recommend the first few years be spent at home in a loving, calm, and secure environment. Sometimes this is impossible. Then extreme care must be exercised in choosing an alternative. Is your day care run by professionals who love and understand children or is it an overcrowded storage place for children? Do you compensate for lack of time with your son by giving quality time when you are together? The child in nursery school can get caught in a vicious cycle of impersonal school and tired working parents. A four-year-old is developing attitudes which can persist for an entire lifetime. Don't let the situation remain as it is. Step in, solve the unhappiness, or make a change.

Q   My child refuses to get dressed in time for school in the morning. He plays and fiddles around and consequently he is frequently late. I try to hurry him along, but unless I dress him myself, he just never is ready on time. What should I do?

A   I would guess the reason for this behavior is because you have always come to his rescue. What would happen if you told him he is on his own and then let him suffer the consequences of being late or missing the school bus? If this isn't practical, set up an appropriate penalty when he is late. Make it reasonable, apply it without anger, but assess the penalty every time he is late. A loss of play time equal to time lost due to tardiness might be a good idea. Make the penalty logical and not excessive so it is not seen as punishment.

Q   My eight-year-old daughter dresses like an urchin. How can I teach her good taste?

A   Don't make too much of an issue of this now. The magic of puberty will work wonders. In the meantime, compliment her (though not effusively or falsely) when she does dress well, and provide her with a good example. Take her shopping with you and help her choose flattering clothes. Let her experience the fun of occasionally dressing up and also the relaxation of being a slob in the privacy of her own home.

Q   My senior-high daughter has begun drinking alcoholic beverages. She becomes hostile when I question her about her behavior. What should I do? She refuses to discuss the subject.

A.   Senior high is late to try to get control. Normally, one month of successful behavior modification is required for every year of lack of control. Use the levers you have. Let her know what you will accept, listen to reasonable suggestions from your daughter, and be willing to negotiate where possible. Once the rules are established, enforce them without exception. Ignore threats but be prepared to have them carried out at least temporarily. Stick to your guns.

Q My elementary child is behind in reading and I would like to help him at home. What can I do? I'm a working mother and don't have much extra time.

A Reading to a child is a great way to stimulate reading interest. Your child's problem must receive high priority, so whatever time you have, read to and with your child. Ask his teacher for advice, particularly about books which are appropriate to the school program. If possible, get the reading book used by the class and read this to him to give him familiarity. Barring physical problems, reading is mostly psychological. Confidence leads to success and success builds confidence. I hope your school also recognizes this and protects the children who are physically immature so that self-images are not damaged during the lag in physical development. Don't rub the sore spot by requiring oral reading of difficult material. This just reinforces the poor self-image. Read to the child and read aloud in unison with him to increase familiarity and confidence.

Additional Readings

Brazelton, T. Berry, M.D. *Toddlers and Parents*. Delacorte
    Press, 1974.
Cahoon, Owen W.; Price, Alvin H.; Scoresby, A. Lynn.
    Parents and the Achieving Child. Provo, Utah:
    Brigham Young University Press, 1979.
Denzin, Norman K. *Childhood Socialization*.
    San Francisco: Jossey-Bass, Publishers, 1979.
Di Leo, Joseph H. *Child Development: Analysis and
    Synthesis*. New York: Brunner/Mazel.
Dill, John R. *Child Psychology in Contemporary
    Society*. Boston: Allyn and Bacon, 1978.
Dworetzky, John P. *Introduction to Child Development*.
    New York: West Publishing Company, 1984.
Elkind, David. *A Sympathetic Understanding of the Child
    Six to Sixteen*. Boston: Allyn and Bacon, 1971.
_____*Children and Adolescents,* 2nd Ed. New York:
    Oxford University Press, 1974.
_____*The Child and Society*. New York: Oxford
    University Press, 1979.
Fitzwater, Ivan W. *Failproof Children*. San Antonio:
    Mandel Publications, 1979.
Freeman, Joan. *Gifted Children*. Baltimore: University
    Park Press, 1979.
Gordon, Thomas. *Parent Effectiveness Training*.
    New York: Peter H. Wyden, Inc., 1970.

Grey, Loren, Ph.D. *Discipline Without Fear*. New York: Hawthorn Books, Inc., 1974.

Gruenberg, Sidonie Mastner. *The Parents' Guide to Everyday Problems of Boys and Girls*. New York: Random House, 1958.

Hooks, William H. (Ed.). *The Pleasure of Their Company*. Radnor, PA: Chilton Book Company, 1981.

Miezio, Peggy Mueler. *Parenting Children with Disabilities*. New York: Dekker, Inc., 1983.

Olen, Dale R. *Teaching Life Skills to Children*. New York: Paulist Press, 1984.

Stevens, Suzanne H. *The Learning Disabled Child: Ways That Parents Can Help*. Winston-Salem: John F. Blair, Publisher, 1980.